Easter Programs for the Church

#10

compiled

Laurie Hoard

cover photo by

Colour Library International

STANDARD PUBLISHING
Cincinnati, Ohio   8722

ISBN 0-87403-082-X

CONTENTS

Easter

Mother's Day

Father's Day

Pentecost

It Was for Us

Marlene Bagnull

Multimedia Experience of Christ's Passion

Introduction:

The script for "It Was for Us" provides a commentary by eyewitness news reporters of the events happening in Jerusalem during the Passover of A.D. 32. Both participants and observers will be enabled to enter more fully into this experience of Christ's passion through the use of the special music and audio-visual aids that are suggested.

The special music might be provided by a soloist, quartet, youth or adult choir. The hymns listed are merely suggestions. Feel free to substitute other selections which may be more readily available to you, or which you feel would have more meaning to your congregation.

The use of the audio-visual aids is entirely optional and should be decided upon the basis of resources you have accessible to you through congregational members or a local audio-visual lending library.

While suggestions are given in the script for the use of a recording, no suggestions are given for the use of slides and filmstrips. You will need to determine for yourself where to best use whatever slides and filmstrips you are able to obtain.

There is no staging necessary beyond the dimming of lights in your sanctuary or church hall. Neither are costumes needed, as the focus of the audience will be on the slides and filmstrips you are projecting.

One or two rehearsals to coordinate the use of the audio-visual resources should be all that are necessary. Be sure to choose good readers who are gifted to portray emotion. This drama can be most effectively presented as a part of a Good Friday service.

Participants:

Amos Ben Zadok, anchorman
Benjamin Bar Jacob, Sanhedrin member
Nathaniel Absalom, reporter
John, the disciple
Nicodemus, Sanhedrin member
Marcus, a Roman physician
Jesus

Special Music *(by soloist, quartet, youth or adult choir):*

" 'Tis Midnight; and on Olive's Brow"
"What Will You Do With Jesus?"
"O Sacred Head, Now Wounded"
"Beneath the Cross of Jesus"
"What Wondrous Love Is This"

Audio-Visual Aids:

Slides of art masterpieces of Christ's passion
Filmstrips showing the various scenes described
"The Whipping" from album *Barabbas* (optional)
Hammer
Crown of thorns, whip, nails, and mallet

Suggested Worship Outline

Organ Prelude

Call to Worship
"Jesus ... though he was God, did not demand and cling to his rights as God, but laid aside his mighty power and glory, taking the disguise of a slave and becoming like men. And he humbled himself even further, going so far as actually to die a criminal's death on a cross. Yet it was because of this that God raised him up to the heights of heaven and gave him a name which is above every other name, that at the name of Jesus every knee shall bow in heaven and on earth and under the earth, and every tongue shall confess that Jesus Christ is Lord, to the glory of God the Father" (Philippians 2:6-11, *The Living Bible).*

Hymn: "Were You There?"

Dramatic Presentation: "It Was for Us"

Scripture Reading: Isaiah 53:3-12

Our Response
Use the quietness of these moments to meditate on all you have seen and experienced. *(Note: During this time you may wish to silently pass through the congregation a crown of thorns, whip, nails, and mallet.)*

Spontaneous Prayers and Pastoral Prayer

Hymns of Commitment: "My Faith Looks Up to Thee" and "All to Jesus I Surrender"

Closing Benediction: Hebrews 12:2-4, 12, 13

Solo: "When I Survey the Wondrous Cross"

It Was for Us

AMOS BEN ZADOK: Good evening. This is Amos Ben Zadok of station WJER in Jerusalem. As you know, we have been closely following the activities of the rabbi from Nazareth since He entered the city last Sunday accompanied by an exuberant procession of His followers. Tonight, behind closed doors, Jesus and His disciples celebrated the Passover feast. It is rumored that Jesus departed from the age-old rituals, and passed around a cup of wine and loaf of bread as symbolic representations of His body and blood. While no one is certain what Jesus meant by this, one thing is certain—tonight in Jerusalem, tension and tempers are at a crisis point. A confrontation between Jesus and the temple authorities is likely to occur very soon.

Here with us in our studio is Benjamin Bar Jacob, an influential member of the Sanhedrin. Benjamin, we know that the temple authorities have set themselves against Jesus. This is difficult for many of the common people to understand, for they have known Jesus to be a kindly man who has responded in seemingly miraculous ways to the needs of many people. Could you please explain the temple's position to us?

BENJAMIN BAR JACOB: It is indeed a pleasure to be with you tonight and to expose this Jesus as the fraud He really is. He has made such ridiculous claims to divinity that I fail to see how any faithful Jew can take Him seriously. He has made a practice of breaking the Sabbath laws, and He has even had the audacity to be the guest in the home of a despised tax collector. We can no longer tolerate His disrespect of our ancient and sacred laws, or His mockery of our holy and righteous religious leaders. And now that He has actually been foolish enough to interfere with worship in the temple—

AMOS BEN ZADOK: I assume you are referring to the incident when Jesus drove the money changers and sellers of sacrificial animals out of the temple?

BENJAMIN BAR JACOB: Absolutely. The temple workers are faithful servants of the Most High. They have every right to be outraged at the disgraceful way Jesus disrupted their important religious duties.

AMOS BEN ZADOK: You are doubtlessly aware that many support Jesus' action as brave and noble.

BENJAMIN BAR JACOB (becoming angry): How can they—

AMOS BEN ZADOK: I don't wish to argue this point with you. Besides, I am sure you'll agree that far more important than this controversy is the grave potential for violence that currently exists. Everyone knows that the Romans are just waiting for an opportunity to intervene and call in their troops. Benjamin, what can concerned citizens do? What does the Sanhedrin plan to do?

BENJAMIN BAR JACOB: Well—

AMOS BEN ZADOK: Excuse me. A report is just coming in from one of our reporters, Nathaniel Absalom. We switch to live coverage outside the Garden of Gethsemane.

NATHANIEL ABSALOM: The confrontation has come. The temple authorities and guards, armed with clubs and led by Judas Iscariot—one-time disciple of Jesus—have just placed Jesus under arrest. They have bound Him and roughly dragged Him off to the High Priest's house. There was a brief moment when the violence we had feared nearly developed as one of Jesus' disciples attacked a guard. Jesus, obviously realizing they were outnumbered, told His disciple to put his sword away.

Hey, you there! Wait a minute. Would you please fill us in on what has been happening?

JOHN *(upset and nervous):* We came with Jesus to the garden several hours ago. He seemed almost distraught when He asked us to wait and watch while He went off to pray by himself. And now, my Master, a man of peace—a man who has only sought to lift the burdens of the downtrodden—has been arrested. *(Pauses, struggling to control emotion.)*

Jesus tried to prepare us for this, but we didn't believe Him. Yet tonight at the feast we should have suspected this would soon happen. He was more sorrowful than I have ever seen Him. There seemed to be a note of finality in all He said to us. He came here to pray because He knew this was coming.

NATHANIEL ABSALOM: Well, what good did He think praying would do? Excuse me, I don't mean to be disrespectful of the Most High, but certainly if Jesus knew what was going to happen, wouldn't He have been wise to tell the city or to mobilize His followers to prevent the temple authorities from arresting Him? Certainly with His popularity, He could have found many people who would have been willing to defend Him.

JOHN: You don't understand. My Master is a man of peace. And as for running away—He would never do that! Besides, He has the power to strike down all of His enemies if He wants to. We had once hoped that He would use His power to overthrow the Romans and establish His kingdom, but increasingly He has been telling us that His kingdom is not of this world. Instead He says His kingdom will come through the shedding of His blood. *(Pauses.)* I'm confused and upset by all that has happened here tonight, but of one thing I am certain—Jesus chose to let them take Him captive.

NATHANIEL ABSALOM: Your Jesus is either very brave or very foolish. Certainly He must know what awaits Him at the hands of the Sanhedrin. And if, as you say, He does have the power to strike down His enemies but chooses instead to willingly turn himself over to them, this must have been a most difficult decision to make.

Special Music *(as John speaks):* " 'Tis Midnight; and on Olive's Brow"

JOHN: I have never in the three years I have been with Jesus seen Him like He was tonight. He begged us to stay awake and pray; and then, with slumped shoulders and unsteady legs, He went off by himself. I could still hear and see Him from where I sat. I wanted to run and console Him as He wept and in anguish rocked back and forth. But I felt frightened and overwhelmed. Jesus has always been so strong, His faith in Yahweh so real. I didn't know how to help Him. As He pleaded with His Father to remove what He called the "cup of suffering," I shut my eyes to try and block out the horror of what I was witnessing—of what I feared He might mean. And then, God forgive me, instead of staying awake and praying as He had entreated me to do, I fell asleep.

Jesus returned and awakened me and the others—not just once, but twice. As I looked into His swollen and red eyes, somehow the pain I knew He was experiencing entered me as well. He walked away again, and threw himself on the ground. Again He wept and cried out for help. But then the strength that is my Master's triumphed, as He raised himself to His knees. With arms outstretched, He told His Father that He would accept the cup that was His to bear.

NATHANIEL ABSALOM: We continue our stirring coverage of these events with Amos Ben Zadok who is now in the court-yard of the High Priest's home.

AMOS BEN ZADOK: Jesus has just emerged from behind the closed doors where I am told members of the Sanhedrin had hastily assembled. The interrogation has obviously been very brutal, for Jesus' face is bruised and swollen, and spittle mixed with blood is running down His cheeks. It is said that He has admitted to being the Son of God, and that the High Priest has torn his clothes and pronounced Jesus guilty of blasphemy. Here comes a member of the Sanhedrin who, it is rumored, has been sympathetic to Jesus. Nicodemus, can you confirm what has just taken place?

NICODEMUS: I don't understand—Jesus condemned himself! It was obvious by their contradictory stories that the witnesses were lying. I felt ashamed to be a part of it all. Yet Caiaphas was determined to convict Him. He kept badgering Jesus—shouting at Him and calling Him a fraud.

I wanted to stop it, but I'm only one man. What could I do in the presence of all of His enemies? And when Jesus admitted to being the Messiah—the Son of God—all hope of saving a man whose work and teaching I have come to respect, was lost.

The mighty Sanhedrin has, through a mockery of a trial, convicted Jesus. Yet I cannot help but feel that we were the ones really on trial—especially as Jesus silently bore the abuse that followed His sentencing. They spat in His face. They slapped His face from side to side, reminding Him of His teaching about turning the other cheek. And they didn't stop there. Some of the guards formed a circle around Him. After blindfolding Him, they punched Him and pushed Him around the circle saying, "Prophesy to us, you Messiah! Who struck you this time?"

And I—I did nothing. May the God of my fathers—of Jesus—forgive me.

NATHANIEL ABSALOM: I am standing outside the Fortress Antonia where Jesus has been brought by the temple authorities for the pronouncement and carrying out of the death sentence. Rumor has it that Pontius Pilate is reluctant to grant their request and may hope to save Jesus by having Him scourged instead. Amos Ben Zadok is inside the fortress. We switch to live coverage.

AMOS BEN ZADOK: From where I am standing, I can see the soldiers shoving Jesus into the courtyard. They are stripping Him, and chaining Him to a stone pillar. Now the lictor has moved into position and brought back his whip. It is whistling through the air, and has just struck Jesus' bare back for the first time.

Special Sound Effects: "The Whipping"

AMOS BEN ZADOK: Now the whip is moving in a slow steady rhythm. The skin of Jesus' chest and back is being ripped to shreds. His body is torn with irrepressible shaking. His face is ashen—His lips trembling. His breathing is labored and broken by moans. He must be suffering unbearable pain, and yet He remains silent—no pleas for mercy, or curses on His tormenters.

Marcus, as a physician to the Roman garrison, have you ever seen a man display such extraordinary courage through such a scourging?

MARCUS: I agree with you that this man is indeed remarkable. The punishment He is silently enduring is severe. It is often called the "halfway death," because it is supposed to stop just this side of death. The whip is made of several strips of leather, at the end of which is sewed a chunk of bone or a small piece of iron chain.

AMOS BEN ZADOK: As you know, the sentence of crucifixion is being sought by the temple leaders. Jesus has already suffered greatly. Assuming the sentence is carried out, what further agonies does He face on the cross?

MARCUS: The Romans have perfected the science of crucifixion. It is the slowest and most painful method of punishing criminals ever devised. First of all, Jesus will experience excruciating pain in His hands and feet where the large iron nails will pin Him to the cross. Beyond that, the muscle spasms and cramps in His arms and legs, and pads of His shoulders, will be unbearable. He will not die, however, from these wounds, but rather from asphyxiation. As He hangs from His hands, the pectoral muscles at the sides of His chest will become momentarily paralyzed. He will be forced time after time to raise His body on the nail pounded through His feet, until His chest is even with His outstretched arms and He can again breathe. Then, as the pain in His feet and cramps in His legs and thighs becomes unendurable, He will be forced to let His body sag lower and lower until He is again hanging by the nails through His hands. After hours of repeating this process He will have no strength to raise himself up, and He will die from lack of oxygen.

Special Music: "What Will You Do With Jesus?" (verse 1)

NATHANIEL ABSALOM: I am standing outside the Fortress Antonia where Pilate has just appeared with Jesus. Jesus is wearing a purple robe and crown of thorns. As a concession to the Jews for their Passover feast, Pilate is indicating his willingness to release Jesus or Barabbas—an insurrectionist convicted of murder. I can hardly believe my ears. The mob is screaming for Pilate to crucify Jesus. The man who has helped and healed so many is being condemned, while the murderer is being allowed to go free.

Special Music: "O Sacred Head, Now Wounded" (verse 1)

NATHANIEL ABSALOM: Now as our cameras follow the execution procession to Golgotha, we see Jesus stumble and fall beneath the heavy burden of the cross. The burden He carries, however, must be far beyond the physical dimension. The hatred and rejection He has experienced from the people He said He came to save, must be causing a burden of heartache that is even heavier to carry.

AMOS BEN ZADOK: Nathaniel and I are at Golgotha—the Place of the Skull outside Jerusalem—where the crucifixion of Jesus of Nazareth is about to take place. This is without a doubt the most difficult assignment I have ever covered. I have followed Jesus' activities throughout His career—I have witnessed the countless times He has healed the sick, given comfort to the sorrowing, and food to the hungry. Always I have seen Him give of himself for others. And now He stands quietly with His head bowed prepared to make the ultimate sacrifice. I have not understood His politics, but perhaps that is because His kingdom truly is not of this world as He told Pilate.

NATHANIEL ABSALOM: They have stripped Jesus and thrown Him down upon the cross. He is not fighting them, but lies there with His eyes closed and lips moving silently. With a thud *(Sound effect.)* the mallet has been brought down on the nail. Still there is no screaming as the nail rips through the flesh and bone—first of His left hand, then His right. Now two soldiers have grabbed the cross and are lifting it up, dragging Jesus by the nails in His hands. With every breath He is groaning. The cross is jolted down into the hole. Again you can hear *(Sound effect.)* the thud of the hammer as His feet are nailed into place. Jesus of Nazareth—He who told Caiaphas He was the Son of God—is crucified!

The crowd is responding unmercifully to the sight of Jesus on the cross. With savage sarcasm, they are taunting Him to climb down—to save himself if He is the Messiah as He has proclaimed himself to be.

I had thought myself a hardened reporter, but seeing this man writhe in agony yet still fail to lash out at His enemies. . .

Special Music: "Beneath the Cross of Jesus"

VOICE OF JESUS: Father, forgive them, for they don't know what they are doing.

AMOS BEN ZADOK: The mob is quiet now, stunned by Jesus' words. Fear and uneasiness has seemed to have taken hold of them. The sky is darkening as I have never seen it do at midday. *(Pauses.)*

The increasing darkness is making it difficult to see. Is Jesus dead? No, lightning has just illuminated His figure on the cross. He appears to be straining upwards ... trying to reach for—

VOICE OF JESUS: My God, my God, why have you forsaken me?

AMOS BEN ZADOK: I can't bear to be a witness to His despair and suffering. *(Voice breaks.)* Never have I been so drawn to a man—or is He but a man? What if He really is the Son of God?

Special Music: "What Wondrous Love Is This"

Because You Ask Not

Donna Fletcher Crow

An Audience Participation Drama

Characters:

MARTHA
FRIEND 1
FRIEND 2
FRIEND 3
WOMAN
DEBORAH, teenager
SARI, teenager
RHODA, teenager
ZIPPORAH, adult
LAZARUS
MARY
JOHN DAVID, teenager
JESUS
RACHEL, child
REBECCA, child
MOURNER 1
MOURNER 2
MOURNER 3

Audience Participation Notes

Every effort has been made to involve the audience in this production by making them part of the action. All extra parts are spoken by members of the audience who may be in modern dress—sometimes right from their seats, sometimes taking their seats after their part is played.

The singing is by the congregation, providing a background for their thoughts or comments on the play. Have printed song-sheets in pews to avoid fumbling with hymnals. Song director can stand offstage to direct singing.

Scene 1

Overture by instruments: Medley of "Sitting at the Feet of Jesus," (Mary's theme); "Does Jesus Care?" (Martha's theme); and "Tell It to Jesus."

(Martha enters. She is exhausted. She pauses, looks at audience, pulls herself together and goes down center speaking to congregation.)

MARTHA: Welcome, my friends and neighbors. My sister, Mary, and I deeply appreciate your coming here to inquire about our brother. Lazarus has been ill for many days and yet the sickness lingers. But please try not to worry. He will recover.

(Three friends from audience step forward—may be men or women.)

FRIEND 1 *(steps forward):* Martha, is there anything we can do to be of aid to your household?

MARTHA: Thank you, my friend. But everything that can be done is being attended to. After all, I have had much experience with nursing.

FRIEND 2: Oh yes, your healing skills are as well known as your arts of hostessing and housekeeping. But Martha, Lazarus has been ill for so long, I wondered if—

MARTHA *(stubborn):* He will survive.

FRIEND 1: But I wondered if I might make a suggestion.

MARTHA: Yes, of course.

FRIEND 1: Your friend Jesus has healed so many. We have heard of a paralyzed man in Capernaum who now moves as nimbly as a young boy, and a crippled man at the pool of Bethesda who at the word of Jesus got up and carried his own bed, and just recently, Jesus healed ten lepers near Galilee, and—

MARTHA *(impatiently):* Yes, yes. I have heard of all these miracles and many more. Just what are you getting at?

FRIEND 2: We mean that, since He is your friend and His reputation for healing grows larger each day, we thought you might seek His help for Lazarus.

MARTHA *(annoyed)*: Yes, He is our friend. I have been His hostess when He visits Jerusalem. We have provided Jesus with the nearest thing He has to a home. But that is certainly no reason we should impose on Him.

FRIEND 3: Well, Martha, I must say I agree with you. After all, God knows what you need before you ask—there's no need to go crying to Him with all our problems. It's not only a sign of weakness, but also a sign of lack of faith.

MARTHA: Thank you, my friend. I'm so glad somebody understands how I feel. Remember the woman who was healed just by touching the hem of His garment? She didn't have to ask for anything.

FRIEND 1: It's true, Martha, she didn't *say* anything, but she did *go* to Him.

MARTHA: Oh, I don't know. The more I think about it the more confused I become. But now I really must get back to work.

(Martha turns away, friends return to seats in congregation.)

Song: "Tell It to Jesus," (chorus only)

(During song, Martha starts toward door right, sees bench, sinks down exhaustedly. Woman gets up from audience and goes to Martha in a concerned manner.)

WOMAN: Martha, you are so tired. You will be ill, too. *(Sits on bench by Martha.)*

MARTHA: No, no. I'm all right. Don't worry.

WOMAN: Martha, I'm so worried about Lazarus. Will he ... will he ... I mean, what if—

MARTHA *(sharply):* Listen to me! Lazarus has been ill before, as have others of this household. Don't you remember? *(Woman nods.)* And don't you also remember that between your prayers and my nursing they have always recovered? Is this not so?

WOMAN: But Martha, the sickness has never been so bad before.

MARTHA: No! It will be as before. You'll see. *(Martha turns away, woman touches her shoulder.)*

WOMAN: But, but ... Martha, will you send for Him?

MARTHA: Send for Him? What are you talking about?

WOMAN: Martha, you *know* what I'm talking about.

MARTHA: I'm sorry, I'm far too busy to discuss all this. But, no, I do *not* plan to send for the Master. *(Stands.)*

WOMAN *(standing):* But, Martha, did you consider that you'll hurt Him if you shut Him out now? He loves you, He would *want* to help—if only you'd ask.

MARTHA: I'm doing all that can be done. We gather fresh herbs twice a day, I keep cool cloths on his fevered brow, he is given sips of water regularly, I feed him fresh broth . . . what more do you expect of me?

WOMAN: But Martha, that's just the point. We can't rely on what we can do—we must rely on what God can do.

MARTHA: Are you suggesting I should just sit down and let God take over? I'm sorry, but that doesn't make sense to me. I believe He gave me a job to do and I intend to do it with every ounce of strength I have.

WOMAN: But—

MARTHA: No! *(Softer, with hand on woman's shoulder.)* Something *you* haven't considered is that Jesus is facing great adversity right now. We have no right to add to His burdens. Why, we have heard that just a few days ago He narrowly escaped being stoned to death in Jerusalem. It is not safe for Him to be in Judea. What if His intervention for us should cause the authorities to take steps to silence Him? Permanently. It is not thinkable. I cannot consider it. I will not consider it. *(Martha dismisses woman who goes back to seat in audience. Martha stands a moment in dejection.)*

Song: "What a Friend We Have in Jesus" (last two lines of verse 1)

MARTHA *(walking down aisle and speaking to people in audience):* You, Deborah, I have need of cool water in my brother's room. Go draw some at the well.

DEBORAH *(jumps up):* Yes, Mistress. *(Hurries out the aisle.)*

MARTHA: Sari, go to the kitchen and bring a basin of fresh broth. And don't spill any.

SARI: I'll hurry, Mistress. *(Runs out.)*

MARTHA: Rhoda, I cannot find my sister anywhere. Please find her and tell her I need her help. Quickly.

18

RHODA: I will, Mistress Martha. *(Goes out. Martha continues down aisle and starts speaking to another servant.)*

ZIPPORAH *(from behind curtain):* Martha! Martha! Come quickly! Martha!

Scene 2

(Martha gathers up her skirts, rushes up the aisle to the stage. As Martha runs, a curtain across center of stage is opened to reveal Lazarus' room. Lazarus is on his pallet up center. He is laying in a strangely twisted position and seems not to be breathing.)

MARTHA *(clamps hand over Zipporah's mouth):* Zipporah, what is the matter with you? Be quiet!

ZIPPORAH *(steps back to clutch doorpost):* Lazarus! He's, he's— *(Points to Lazarus.)*

MARTHA *(runs to pallet, kneels by Lazarus and gently straightens him in bed, places hand on his forehead and then feels chest for pulse):* Zipporah! Be quiet! I need you to help me. Bring me that cushion.

ZIPPORAH *(moves slowly to bring pillow):* But . . . but isn't he . . . dead?

MARTHA: No. It seems a miracle, but he is alive. And we must see to his needs.

(Deborah and Sari enter with jug of water and large bowl of broth. Zipporah dips cloth in water, wrings it out, and brings it to Martha.)

Song: "Does Jesus Care?" (verse 1 [no chorus] behind action, instruments continue through next speech.)

(Zipporah picks up used rags and exits.)

MARTHA: My God, my God, where are You? I have worked so hard. I've done all I could do. No, I've done more than anyone could. What more can I do? What do you want of me? Dear God, there is nothing in my world but sickness and death and

I can't do anything about it. How long, oh Lord, how long must this go on?

Music: A few bars of "Sitting at the Feet of Jesus" softly, as Mary enters.

MARY: You sent for me?

MARTHA: Mary! Where have you been? Of course I sent for you! I needed you. Why do you always disappear when I've so much work to do? Where were you?

MARY: I climbed the hill behind our house to my special place. I wanted to think about Jesus and the times He has spent with us—the time I have spent sitting at His feet. I wanted to recall the stories He told and the questions He answered. I depend on Him.

MARTHA *(sarcastically):* Well, I'm sure that sounds absolutely lovely. But what would happen if we all spent our time sitting on a hillside meditating? You never think of the work there is to be done.

MARY: My sister, I think of work, but it is the work of teaching and healing that Jesus does that I have been thinking of.

MARTHA: And were there any practical results of your lengthy meditations? Did God shed the light of wisdom on our circumstances?

MARY: Oh, yes, Martha, I think it is God's will that we send for Jesus. He said He had come that we might have life and have it more abundantly. Can't that mean physical life as well as spiritual? Lazarus needs Jesus' touch if he is to be well again.

MARTHA: Listen Mary, there should be no need for us to send for Him. As one of our friends reminded me a few minutes ago, He himself said that our Father in Heaven knows our needs before we ask. So if He is God, as He claims, He already knows we need Him. *(Looks at Mary.)* Even with all your holy trustfulness, can you give me one reason why Jesus has not come on His own before this?

Music: Instruments begin "Tell It to Jesus"

MARY: Well, maybe He *wants* us to *ask.* Maybe ... oh, I don't know. All I know is that tonight as I prayed, I felt we should send for the Master. From there, my sister, I just don't know.

Song: "Tell It to Jesus" (verses 1 and 3)

(Martha turns her back on Mary and the audience. On verse 3, she kneels by Lazarus, displaying her agitation. Slowly she goes back to Mary.)

MARTHA *(embraces Mary, crying):* Oh, Mary, I am sorry I was so cross with you. Forgive me. My mind just doesn't seem to be functioning tonight.

MARY: Of course I forgive you. *(Pulling away.)* But aren't you going to send for Jesus? Haven't you heard a word I've said?

MARTHA: Yes Mary, I've heard. But I'm not convinced.

MARY: You weren't so shy about asking Him for help when you wanted me reproved.

MARTHA: Of course, that showed I appreciated His authority. But that doesn't mean we should run to Him every time something goes wrong. And you needn't think you're the only one with any faith just because you want to call for Jesus. It can be an act of faith to believe He'll take care of it without asking.

MARY *(softly):* Yes, Martha. It can be. But *is* it?

MARTHA *(hedging):* Well, there was the centurion's son. He was healed long-distance without Jesus going to him. Remember?

MARY: Yes, but word *was* sent. I think we need to do something to show we believe in Him.

MARTHA: Oh, I just don't know. Nothing seems to make any sense anymore.

MARY *(goes to Martha):* But listen, Martha, He heals multitudes daily. Remember the disciples telling us how people thronged Him? *(Zipporah enters with a pile of clean cloths.)* And He healed them *all.* Why should He do less for His dear friend?

MARTHA: Mary, you—

ZIPPORAH: Forgive me, Mistress, if it weren't for the great love I bear your family I would hold my tongue. But the Master has given us so many teachings that we are *supposed* to ask. Like when He said, "If your son asks for bread, would any of you fathers give him a stone? And—"

MARY: Yes, I remember. "And if he asks for an egg, would you give him a serpent? And just think how much better your heavenly Father loves to give good gifts to his children."

(Martha looks from one to the other desperately, caught be-tween.)

ZIPPORAH: And then there was the story about the man who was out of bread and his neighbor finally gave him some because he asked and asked.

MARY: Martha—

MARTHA: Stop it, both of you! Oh, just leave me alone! *(Runs down the aisle sobbing.)*

Scene 3

(A short time later. Mary sits on a stool in the hall, doing needlework. Martha enters slowly. Mary runs to her.)

MARY: Martha, you've thought it over. You see we were right!

MARTHA *(shakes head):* No, Mary, not at all.

MARY: What is the matter with you? Why do you keep holding out on this? You must think Lazarus' life is too far gone even for Jesus. Don't you realize that isn't possible? Don't you believe the accounts we've heard of Jesus bringing the widow's son back to life in Nain? Or over in Capernaum when He raised Jairus' daughter? What if He is late—is anything too late with God? *(Martha turns away.)* You don't want to ask Jesus to heal Lazarus because you don't think He can do it! You're afraid He'll fail and then you'll be embarrassed.

MARTHA *(angry, grips Mary's shoulders):* That's not true! *(Releases Mary and continues sadly.)* Mary, Mary, I know of Jesus' divine powers. But I also know that I have to be practical. The Scriptures tell us there's a time to be born and a time to die and my dear, if it's Lazarus' time, we must accept the will of God in this. *(Pauses.)* Now, my brother has been unattended far too long. Come with me, Mary.

LAZARUS: Martha, is that you?

MARY: Lazarus! You're awake!

LAZARUS: Yes, I slept very well. And I'm ravenous. Martha, what's going to happen to your reputation for hospitality when it gets out that you've been starving your brother?

MARTHA *(laughing):* Will you promise not to tell if I get you some food very quickly?

22

LAZARUS: A starving man will agree to anything.

MARTHA *(goes to door and calls):* Zipporah! Some bread for my brother!

LAZARUS: Mary, I dreamed that Jesus was here—or was it a dream? Is He here?

MARY: You were dreaming, Lazarus.

LAZARUS: Oh, what a disappointment. I would love to see Him.

MARTHA *(coming back with bread):* Well, then, we'll send for Him. Mary has just been saying we should do that, haven't you?

MARY: Martha!

MARTHA *(goes down center, calls toward audience):* John David! *(A teenage serving boy comes forward.)*

JOHN: Yes, Mistress.

MARTHA: You are to go on an errand. My sister and I want you to take a message to the Master. We have heard that He is in Perea. It is a long journey so you must take provisions. *(Martha ushers him offstage, pantomiming instructions. John David hurries out down the aisle. Martha exits right.)*

MARY *(sits by Lazarus, dipping the bread Zipporah has brought into broth and feeding him):* Just eat it slowly, Lazarus.

LAZARUS: That's enough, thank you, Mary.

MARY: Enough! You only took three bites. I thought you were hungry.

LAZARUS: Maybe I'll have some more later. I'd like to rest now.

MARY: Yes, Brother, you rest and our friends and I will sing for you.

Song: "Is It the Crowning Day?" (verses 1 and 2)

MARY *(to audience):* That was lovely. Thank you so much. I'm sure my brother enjoyed it. Didn't you Lazarus? *(Turns to him.)* Lazarus ... Lazarus! *(Runs offstage.)* Martha!

Scene 4

(Curtain is drawn across Lazarus' room. Mary and Martha wear black veils. Mary is sitting on a stool up center left, Martha on bench, right.)

23

MARY: I don't understand. It doesn't seem possible. He *was* better, Martha. He ate a little broth. Then he wanted to rest and we sang to him. It was lovely. And when it was over . . . he was . . . he was. *(Drops to knees beside Martha.)* Oh, Martha, our brother is dead.

MARTHA: Yes, Mary. He is gone. *(Puts arm around Mary and strokes her hair comfortingly.)* Try to be brave, little one. *(Gently raises Mary and stands.)* Now, I must prepare him for burial.

MARY: Right now?

MARTHA: Certainly. He must be buried before sundown or decay will set in. Besides all in the house will be unclean until it is accomplished. There is so much to do: I must wash his body, anoint him with scented oils, wrap him in strips of linen with fragrant spices . . . can you help me?

MARY: Yes, Martha.

MARTHA: I will need the oil of spikenard. Will you get it for me?

MARY: Yes, of course. Is there something else I might do?

MARTHA: Not just now, thank you. *(Mary exits, Martha sits heavily on stool.)* Maybe I should have sent for Jesus sooner. If I had, would our brother be alive now? I feel such a burden of guilt. Is all this my fault? Oh, I was always so sure of myself—and now I don't seem to know anything. *(Hands in face, sobbing.)*

Song: "Does Jesus Care?" (verse 3, no chorus)

(Lights out.)

Scene 5

(Martha is folding a large basket of clean linen. Mary, sitting on stool, reads aloud from a scroll.)

MARY: "Out of the depths I cry to you, O Lord; O Lord, hear my voice. Let your ears be attentive to my cry for mercy. I wait for the Lord, my soul waits, and in his word I put my hope. My soul waits for the Lord . . . O Israel, put your hope in the Lord, for with the Lord is unfailing love and with him is full redemption." Oh, Martha, isn't that comforting? It makes me feel so much better.

MARTHA (sighs): How easily you are comforted, my contemplative sister. I find it impossible to accept a situation I cannot understand. The psalm I would choose would be, "O Lord, the God who saves me, day and night I cry out before you. For my soul is full of trouble, and my life draws near the grave. Your wrath lies heavily upon me; you have overwhelmed me with all your waves."

MARY (drops scroll and goes to her): Oh, no, sister. We mustn't blame God for our situation. I am sure that—(Zipporah enters.)

ZIPPORAH (nervous): Mistress, I . . . that is . . . I mean—

MARTHA: What is it, Zipporah?

ZIPPORAH: It's John David. He has returned.

MARTHA: Oh good! Perhaps Jesus can explain things to us—make some sense out of Lazarus' death. Well, why are you standing there? Zipporah, go out and meet Him. He is our guest. (Zipporah doesn't move.) Mary, go fetch a basin of water so we may wash the dust of the road from His feet. (Mary starts out.) Zipporah! Go greet the Master as I told you!

ZIPPORAH: That's just the problem—He's not here. He is . . . is not coming.

MARY (turning around): Not coming? What do you mean—not coming?

MARTHA (dismissing Zipporah): All right, thank you.

Music: "Does Jesus Care?" (instrumental behind scene)

MARTHA (rushes to door and yells): John David! Come here! (He runs in, Martha looks him in the eye.) Well?

JOHN DAVID (hangs head): My mistress, I have failed.

MARTHA: You didn't find the Master?

JOHN DAVID: Oh, yes. He was in Perea as you had heard. It was not hard to find Him because of the great crowds around Him.

MARTHA: Well then?

JOHN DAVID: I waited until He finished His teaching. It was wonderful—many believed on Him just while I was there. I heard one man say, "All that John told us about this Man was true—"

MARTHA: John David, my message!

JOHN DAVID: Oh, yes, Mistress. I said, "Sir, you should know that your friend lies ill," just as you told me to.

MARTHA: And what did He reply?

JOHN DAVID: I . . . I'm not sure.

MARTHA: What do you mean, not sure? Couldn't you hear Him?

JOHN DAVID: Oh, yes, I heard Him. I mean, I'm not sure what He meant—

MARTHA: John David, tell me!

JOHN DAVID: Well, He said, "This sickness will not end in death. No, it is for God's glory so that God's Son may be glorified through it."

MARTHA: Not in death! How can this be? Our brother is *dead!* He has lain in his tomb for two days! *(Martha pantomimes conversation with John David.)*

Song: "Does Jesus Care?" (verse 2, no chorus)

MARY *(to John David):* What happened next?

JOHN DAVID: Nothing.

MARTHA: Nothing? Just like that? Nothing?

JOHN DAVID: Well, Jesus turned back to the people crowding around Him and I couldn't see anything else, so I hurried back. I have traveled all night.

MARTHA: All right, you may go. *(John David returns to seat in audience.)* Is it possible? Can Jesus make a mistake?

MARY: Martha, He said we would see the glory of God, so we must trust Him.

MARTHA: How can I have faith in something that doesn't make sense? And after all the work I've gone to preparing for His coming. Even with the burden of burying our brother, I have seen the household swept and scrubbed, I have baked bread and cakes, I have gathered fruits and vegetables—

MARY *(gently):* Martha, you have always worried over so many things, but remember, Jesus told you only a few were really important—really only one, He said.

MARTHA *(ignoring her):* I have been distracted with all my preparations, I wanted everything to be so special for Him, to show how much I loved Him, and He isn't even coming.

MARY *(softly):* Perhaps you have lost your peace of mind because you emphasize the wrong things.

MARTHA *(going on, as if to herself)*: And after all I've done for Him, too. Not just this time, but in the past. You'd think He could at least send a message that made sense even if He couldn't come. I mean, think of all the dinners I've prepared for Him, always provided a room—

MARY: Martha, He doesn't want your effort. He wants your faith.

Scene 6

(Martha enters up the aisle, speaking to servants sitting in the audience.)

MARTHA: Rhoda, what are you doing in the garden? Didn't I tell you I wanted that wheat ground into flour in time to bake bread for the evening meal?

RHODA: Yes, Mistress. Forgive me. *(Runs up aisle into house.)*

MARTHA: Sari, Deborah, why are you gossiping here instead of seeing to your work? Deborah, there are three baskets of fresh figs to be laid out to dry. Sari, I want all the upstairs carpets beaten. Get Zipporah to help you.

SARI AND DEBORAH: Yes, Mistress. *(They scurry off. As Martha reaches stage, Zipporah runs in from offstage.)*

ZIPPORAH: Mistress, Mistress, He is here! I mean, He's coming! I saw Him down the road.

MARTHA: Zipporah, calm down. Who is here?

ZIPPORAH: HE! The Master. Jesus.

MARTHA: What? Has He come at last?

ZIPPORAH: Yes, yes, it's true.

MARTHA: Go tell my sister. *(Zipporah exits.)*

(Instruments begin "Does Jesus Care?" Martha smooths headpiece and skirt. Jesus enters quietly.)

MARTHA: Master! *(Runs to Jesus, speaks accusingly.)* If you had been here, Lord, my brother would not have died! *(Kneels.)* But I know that even now, whatever You ask of God, He will grant You. Oh, My Lord, You are the only one I can turn to. All my life everyone has turned to me—my brother, my sister, all our household and neighbors.

27

JESUS (holding hand out to Martha): Martha, Your brother will rise again.

MARTHA (takes Jesus' hand and stands): Yes, Lord. I know that he will rise again in the resurrection on the last day.

Music: Instruments begin "Trust in the Lord"

JESUS: I am the resurrection and the life. He who believes in me will live even though he dies. (Pantomime talking behind song.)

Song: "Trust in the Lord" (verse 3)

JESUS: Do you believe this, Martha?

MARTHA: Lord, I do! I now believe that You are the Messiah, the Son of God who was to come into the world.

JESUS: Go call your sister.

(Instruments begin "Sitting at the Feet of Jesus" as Mary enters.)

MARTHA (runs to Mary): The Master is here; He is asking for you.

MARY (runs to Jesus, flings herself at His feet, weeping): Oh, Lord, if you had only been here my brother would not have died.

(Jesus pulls Mary, sobbing, to her feet and puts his arm around her.)

JESUS: Where have you laid him?

Music: "Be Still, My Soul" (instrumental behind scene)

MARTHA: This way, Lord. Come and see. (Martha points to tomb, Mary and Martha follow Jesus up center to tomb. Jesus is weeping.)

RACHEL (from audience): It's Jesus! Remember when He told us a story! (Starts to run to Him.)

REBECCA: Rachel, don't bother Him now!

RACHEL: It's all right, Rebecca.

REBECCA: Wait! *(Grabs her and they stand aside.)*

MOURNER 1 *(from audience):* Look, He is weeping. How dearly He must have loved him.

MOURNER 2 *(from audience, coming forward):* Yes, He was very close to the whole family.

MOURNER 1 *(mourners go to stage, stand down right):* That's true. His tears prove it.

MOURNER 3 *(from audience):* Could not this man, who opened the blind man's eyes, have done something to keep Lazarus from dying?

JESUS *(steps up to tomb):* Take away the stone. *(Mourners 1 and 2 start to push the stone. Martha interrupts.)*

MARTHA: Lord, wait! He has been there four days. By now there will be a terrible stench.

JESUS: Martha, did I not tell you that if you have faith you will see the glory of God? This illness is part of God's plan for the unfolding of His message.

Song: "Be Still, My Soul" (verse 2)

(During song all extras take places on stage, and Jesus pantomimes conversation with Martha.)

JESUS *(waiting):* Martha?

MARTHA: Do as He said. Remove the stone.

(Jesus walks to entrance of tomb. Everyone else draws back, but watches intently.)

JESUS *(toward audience):* Father, I thank You. You have heard me. I knew already that You always hear me, but I speak for the sake of the people standing around, that they might believe that You sent me.

(Martha and Mary stand with arms around each other.)

Music: Instruments begin "Rejoice, the Lord Is King"

JESUS *(facing tomb, calls loudly):* Lazarus, come forth!

(Jesus steps aside and everyone leans forward. Lazarus, wrapped in grave clothes, appears at entrance.)

MOURNERS *(gasp audibly):* It is a spirit? Look—look! He moved! The body moved!

JESUS: Unbind him. Let him go.

MARTHA *(rushes to Lazarus):* Lazarus, Lazarus! You are alive! Can it be?

LAZARUS: Yes, Martha, it is I. Praise God!

MARTHA *(to audience):* It is our brother who was dead and is alive again! *(Martha begins unwinding grave clothes, Mary falls at Jesus' feet.)*

MOURNERS: Hosannah! Praise the Lord! It's a miracle—we've seen a miracle! He must be the Son of God!

Song: Actors sing "Rejoice, the Lord Is King" (verses 1 and 2)

Curtain

Joy to the World

Carol Ely

(Sing to the tune, "Joy to the World")

Joy to the world, the Lord arose!
No longer in death's grave!
He died on the cross
That we may live.
And now He lives again,
Oh, yes, He lives again!
He lives, He lives, He lives again!

Even the stones cry out with joy,
"Behold, the Savior lives!"
No more shall sin or sorrow reign—
He's overcome the world!
He's overcome the world!
He lives, He lives, He lives again!

The Wardrobe of a King

Trudy Keiter

A Biblical Fashion Show

Why at this particular time of the year
Do we feel the great need to display
All newly acquired apparel
Just because it's Easter Day?

I wonder if such attention was paid
To fashion design in the past.
If we had a Biblical fashion show,
How long do you think it would last?

Let's use Jesus as our subject;
Let's examine the clothes that He wore.
Did what He wear connect Him
With the rich or with the poor?

Did He place His primary emphasis
On the way He looked and dressed?
Or was it more important for Him
To live and do His best?

May the following events help lead us
To understand a little more
That the wonderful Easter tradition
Didn't originate in a store.

For there's something more important
To be considered at this time;
Would I be willing to make the very first
Easter wardrobe mine?

A New Wardrobe

He was clothed with strength and majesty.
He lived, enthroned on high.
But because of His love for sinful man,
He chose to say good-bye ...

To the riches of His Heaven,
To the honor due His name,
To the crown of glory that He wore,
That He might man reclaim.

He arose from His throne in glory,
Stripped himself of His robes of light.
And then clothing himself with our nature,
He came to our world one night.

He traded His Heavenly wardrobe
For the garments of poverty.
Wrapped in swaddling clothes, in a manger He lay
When He came to earth for me.

He grew up in a common home,
He wore just common clothes.
He traded His Heavenly raiment
For a robe of earthly woes.

The Layette of a King

She was to bring forth royalty;
That thought made her glad heart sing.
But then Mary began to wonder
How she'd dress her baby King.

She knew that He should have the best
That worldly wealth could buy.
Then she thought of her own poverty
And it made her sad heart cry.

But with loving hands she labored,
Tearing cloth in tiny strips
That would keep her baby safely warmed
From nighttime's chilling grip.

She packed them away so gently,
Not expecting that one day
She'd put her swaddling clothes to use
In a manger bed of hay.

What she lacked in worldly wealth
Was really never needed.
For Jesus grew up happy,
Without ever feeling cheated.

Towel of Humility

He put on the garb of a servant.
He wore the towel of humility
When He laid aside His garments
And washed His disciples' feet.

There kneeling in that upper room,
A Heavenly creator designed
A brand new style of spiritual attire
That's still unique and hard to find.

How many towels have *you* seen today?
Did you wear one for a friend?
If you said, "Yes," then I'll suggest
You'd better look again.

Because there's something very different
About this spiritual accessory.
If you think you're wearing it, you've already lost
Your towel of humility.

The Robe of Stripes

Christ stood in Pilate's judgment hall
On trial, He stood accused
For claiming that He was the long-awaited
Spiritual King of the Jews.

And that He wore a robe of strips
Upon His bleeding back.
And a brand new stripe was added each time
The whip of scourging cracked.

And oh, the pain brought on Him
By that garment that He wore,
The robe of stripes that left His flesh
Hanging open, bleeding and torn.

Robe of Royalty

With the robe of stripes still clinging
To His torn and bleeding back,
The mocking soldiers realized
There was something Jesus lacked.

They realized that this "so-called King"
Was without official array.
So they placed a purple robe on Him
And continued their mocking play.

A Kingly Crown

And Pilate's cruel soldiers
Wanted to make this King complete.
They wanted Him to be royally dressed
From His head down to His feet.

So, they gathered thorns, all razor sharp
And with them made a crown
Then, mocking Him, they placed it
On His head and shoved it down.

The thorns, they pierced His precious brow
And blood streamed down His face.
And my sin was the reason why
He was crowned with such disgrace.

A Robe of Shame

He was stripped of all His garments
And His kingly dignity
When He was called upon to bear the pain
Of Calvary's cruel tree.

Suspended there between earth and sky
He wore only a robe of shame
While heartless soldiers divided His clothes
'Neath His cross in a gambling game.

The Robe of Death

The life drained from His body,
"Forgive them," was His cry.
And after hours of torture,
He bowed His head and died.

A secret friend begged Pilate
For the body of God's Son.
And he, with the help of another, made sure
His burial was speedily done.

They wrapped Him in the robes of death,
Covering up the robe of shame,
Also covering the robe of stripes
That He wore when He bore my blame.

With tender hands they wrapped His flesh
In linen burial strips.
But the love they showed Him was no match
For death's terrible, chilling grip.

They placed His lifeless body
In a dark and lonely tomb
And for three days He lay wrapped in death
Within the cold earth's womb.

A Robe of Victory

And then it happened—the third day came,
And since then nothing has been the same.

For Jesus laid death's garment down;
A robe of victory had been found.

And Jesus left that cold, dark tomb,
Triumphant over Satan's doom.

He conquered sin, He conquered death,
When He arose and breathed new breath.

The robe of victory that He wore
Did not erase the marks He bore.

But, I think He left them there for me,
So that I could see them eternally.

So that I could thank Him o'er and o'er
For the pain He suffered and the robes He wore.

The Robe of Power

Still dressed in garments of victory,
He appeared to His good friends occasionally.

Until He said, "It's time to go,
And soon the third person of God you'll know."

He left this earth all clothed in power,
And He's returning in some unknown hour.

And He'll be dressed in victory
And power and glory for all to see.

He wants to share His robe of power
With all of you this very hour.

So won't you give your life today,
To walk the straight and narrow way?

One Accessory

There's just one accessory He'd have us wear;
One part of His wardrobe that He would share.

Not the robe of stripes or thorny crown,
Not the robe of death left in the ground.

Very simply, He want us to wear His name,
That we might His good news proclaim ...

That He has triumphed over Satan's power
And we can take refuge within His tower.

And some sweet day on Heaven's shore,
We can share His victory forevermore.

An Easter Wardrobe

We've looked at an Easter wardrobe today.
How many of you would like to say
That you would trade your brand new clothes
For one of the robes that Jesus chose
To wear when He left Heaven's glory behind?
When you choose a new wardrobe, keep His in mind!

From the Cradle to the Cross

Linda F. Mouat

A Bible-times Play

Cast:

STORYTELLER
HERALD
EIGHT CHILDREN—two each of different nationalities, repre-
  senting different parts of the world
MARY
JOSEPH
JESUS
PETER
JOHN
JAMES
ANDREW
MARY MAGDALENE
SALOME
MARY, mother of James

Musicians:

ADULT SINGERS (three or more)
CHILDREN'S CHOIR (preschool age and up)
MALE VOCAL SOLOIST
INSTRUMENTAL SOLOIST (any instrument desired)

Props:

cradle
baby (or doll)
three small ointment jars
low stool for Mary
low stool for Storyteller

Settings:

Scene 1: the stable
Scenes 2 and 3: the tomb with the cross in background

Notes:

The Storyteller and the multinational children are seated between and in front of the two settings.

The children's choir may be seated on the floor to one side of the Storyteller. They stand when singing.

The adult singers are seated to one side, standing when they sing.

If the children's choir sings too softly, the adult singers and multinational children may sing with them from where they are seated.

An organist or pianist is needed for musical portions.

Playing time: 30-40 minutes

Scene 1

(As the scene opens, Mary, Joseph, and baby are in the darkened stable. The Storyteller is seated on a low stool, facing the audience.)

STORYTELLER: In those days Caesar Augustus issued a decree that a census should be taken of the entire Roman world. . . . And everyone went to his own town to register. So Joseph also went up from the town of Nazareth in Galilee to Judea, to Bethlehem the town of David, because he belonged to the house and line of David. He went there to register with Mary, who was pledged to be married to him and was expecting a child (Luke 2:1, 3-5).

Adult singers: "We've a Story to Tell to the Nations" (verse 1 and chorus)

(During the chorus, the multinational children enter in pairs from the back of the room. The Herald leads them. They walk up

40

the center aisle and seat themselves in a semicircle in front of the Storyteller facing him/her.)

THE HERALD *(standing and facing the audience):* There was a tiny baby, born in a stable. The Son of God, the Bible says, came to earth that day. So come with me and we will see the story as it unfolds; the fulfillment of God's plans, just as the ancient prophets foretold.

(Organ plays a couple of lines of "Silent Night" as the Herald is seated, facing the Storyteller. Lights on manger scene.)

MARY *(sitting by cradle):* Oh Joseph, I was so afraid when you told me we had to stay here in this stable. When the baby was coming, I just wanted to go home.

JOSEPH *(standing near her):* I'm sorry I couldn't get a room for you, Mary. Everyone has come to be registered, just like us, and there wasn't anyplace else to stay.

MARY: Everything is better now that the baby's been born. He's so healthy and the noises the animals make don't seem to bother Him at all.

JOSEPH *(moving to door or window to look at the sky):* Come over here and look. *(Mary goes to stand with him.)* See how bright the stars are tonight? They remind me of what the shepherds said when they came to see the baby the other night. They told us that a great crowd of angels appeared to them and made the whole night sky light up. When I look at the stars shining, it's easy to imagine the sky filled with God's angels.

MARY: Who could even have dreamed of such a thing! God's angels rejoicing over the birth of this one small baby. *(She goes back to the baby.)* Do you think He looks like the Son of God? The angel who told me I was to have Him said He would be a great king. He doesn't look like a king to me. He's so small and helpless.

JOSEPH: I know. *(He moves to her side.)* The angel who talked to me when you were pregnant said to name the baby, "Jesus." He told me that Jesus will save the people from their sins. But I wonder ... how do you suppose one tiny baby can save anyone from sin?

41

(Lights shift to children's choir. Mary, Joseph and baby exit.)

Children's choir: "Away in a Manger" (verses 1 and 2)

STORYTELLER: When the time of their purification according to the Law of Moses had been completed, Joseph and Mary took him to Jerusalem to present him to the Lord ... and to offer a sacrifice in keeping with what is said in the Law of the Lord: "a pair of doves or two young pigeons." When Joseph and Mary had done everything required by the Law of the Lord, they returned to Galilee to their own town of Nazareth. And the child grew and became strong; he was filled with wisdom, and the grace of God was upon him (Luke 2:22, 24, 39, 40).

Scene 2

(Lights on multinational children. They stand, by nationality, two by two and speak in unison. As one pair finishes, the next pair stands. They face the audience as they speak.)

TWO CHILDREN: Jesus grew up and started His ministry. He asked ordinary men, fishermen, and tax collectors to work with Him. He traveled all over the land.

TWO CHILDREN: Everywhere He went, He healed the sick people. He raised people from the dead. He performed miracles like feeding thousands of people from a meal meant for one.

(Jesus, Peter, John, Andrew, and James enter, seating themselves in a group, while next pair speaks.)

TWO CHILDREN: With power, He drove demons out of people. He caused storms to stop!

TWO CHILDREN: Jesus told everyone the good news of the kingdom of God.

HERALD *(stands, faces audience, acting puzzled):* But what is the good news of the kingdom of God? Does anyone know?

Children's choir: "Tell Me the Story of Jesus" (verse 1)

STORYTELLER: Once when Jesus was praying in private and His disciples were with Him, He asked them ...

(Lights on Jesus and disciples.)

JESUS: Who do the crowds say I am? (Luke 9:18)
ANDREW: John the Baptist—
JAMES: Some say Elias—
JOHN: Others say that one of the prophets is risen again!
  (Short pause.)
JESUS: But what about you? Who do you say I am?
PETER *(with excitement):* The Christ of God!

(Light shifts to adult singers.)

Adult singers: "We've a Story to Tell to the Nations" (verse 3 and chorus)

(Jesus and disciples exit. Light on the Storyteller.)

Scene 3

STORYTELLER: The leaders of the people feared and hated Jesus. They made plans to have Him killed. Bribing one of His disciples, Judas Iscariot, to help them, they came in the night and took Him prisoner. Beaten and treated with cruelty, He was shuffled from official to official until at last He ended up in the court of the Roman governor, Pontius Pilate. Pilate had nothing against Jesus and tried to set Him free. But the people, led by the Jewish leaders, demanded that He be executed. At last, giving in to the pressure, Pilate sent Jesus away to be crucified on a wooden cross, next to two thieves.

Instrumental solo: "The Old Rugged Cross" (one verse)

MULTINATIONAL CHILDREN *(standing together and facing audience):* They've killed God's Son! He's dead!
HERALD *(loudly):* Oh no! Now we will never know what the good news of the kingdom of God is!

(Children are seated.)

43

STORYTELLER: Jesus Christ, the Son of God, hung dead on a cross. That evening, Joseph, a rich man from Arimathea, went to Pilate to ask if he could take away the body of Jesus. Pilate gave his permission. Joseph loved Jesus and tenderly wrapped His body in clean linen. He laid Him in a newly made tomb. No burial could take place on the Sabbath, which was the next day, so to keep intruders out of the tomb, Joseph had a large stone rolled in front of the entrance.

(Light on three women as they enter, holding jars of ointment.)

MARY MAGDALENE: If we hurry, we can anoint our Lord's body and have Him ready for burial before the sun is up.
SALOME: Look! *(Pointing to tomb.)* Someone has rolled the stone away from the door!
MARY, mother of James *(stoops to look in tomb):* Someone has taken His body away! Quickly, run and get Peter and John!

(Salome hurries offstage, returning with the disciples.)

PETER *(addressing the women):* What is this nonsense about His body not being here? I saw Joseph put Him in this tomb myself!

(John bends to look inside tomb while Peter enters tomb.)

JOHN: He's not here! He's gone!

(The women and disciples sit down, facing the Storyteller. The lights dim.)

Vocal solo: "He's Alive" by Don Francisco *(Sheet music available from Alexandria House, Box 300, Alexandria, IN 46001.)*

HERALD *(with great excitement):* That's it! The good news of the kingdom of God is forgiveness from sin!
STORYTELLER: Jesus says in Matthew, chapter 11, "Come to me, all you who are weary and burdened, and I will give you rest. Take my yoke upon you and learn from me, for I am gentle and humble in heart, and you will find rest for your souls."

(The entire cast comes and stands together with the children's choir and the adult singers. Storyteller and children stand.)

All: "We've a Story to Tell to the Nations" (verse 4 and chorus)

STORYTELLER: "For all have sinned and fall short of the glory of God." These words are as true today as they were two thousand years ago when the apostle Paul wrote them to the church in Rome. We need a Savior; someone to take the punishment for our sins and to make a way for us to approach God. The Christ of the cradle became for us the Christ of the cross. He took on himself God's punishment for every sin we would ever commit. The only thing He requires of us is that we accept the sacrifice He made for our salvation. Thank you for sharing with us the good news of the kingdom of God. As we join together and sing "Joy to the World," (page 30) let us each humbly bow our hearts before the Son of God, Jesus Christ.

Curtain

Sonrise

Barbara J. Ritchey

A Reading

Dawn was quietly approaching, sending an occasional stream of gray to pierce the darkness, as she rose from her bed after another futile attempt to sleep. Her eyes were red and swollen as she shuffled to the little wood table and sank into a chair beside it. From there she could look out a small window to the hill overlooking the city.

In the darkness of the early morning she could see only stars and the faint outline of the house next door. The silent peacefulness of the hour reminded her of the night her son had been born. She felt so old and stiff now to have been so very young then.

Such joy ... the softness of His skin ... the evenness of His breathing ... she smiled through her tears at the memory of His crawling days, His first steps, His long lashes caressing His cheeks while He slept.

The memory faded and she rubbed the tears from her face. How could she possibly have any tears left? She had thought she had surely cried them all out by now. The aching within her would not cease. She had lived with fear's fingers clutched tightly around her heart for so many years now—ever since the Wise-men had come with their gifts. The one had brought myrrh ... the spice for the dead. The realization that all the prophecies she had grown up with were now about to take place had shocked her and terrified her.

She sighed and stared at the little box sitting on the table. For over thirty years she had carried the box among her possessions as a reminder of those prophecies, although they lived constantly in her consciousness and needed no reminding. She toyed with the box for a moment and then slowly lifted its lid. It still carried the scent of the spice, but the myrrh was gone—given to the women who would be wrapping the body this very morning. She replaced the lid and gently set the box back on the table.

This time she did nothing to stop the sobs that shook her shoulders as she buried her face in her hands and wept in grief.

If only she could understand ... why did He have to die? What was the purpose of it all to end this way? She prayed for a release from the memories that burned in her mind and would not go away. He had suffered so much before the end had blessedly come. He had been so cruelly tormented. He had been beaten and spat upon. He had been flogged and stripped. Each blow had sent spears of fire through her heart. The soldiers had put thorns on His head that caused great drops of blood to flow down His face. A purple robe had been put over His shoulders in mockery; He had been so weak that the weight of the robe had nearly been too heavy for Him. And then, He had been forced to carry His own cross through the scathing mob until finally He had collapsed onto the rocky pavement.

She would never forget the horror of those hours as she watched her son dying slowly on a cross before her. This child whom she had given birth to, had nurtured, and loved so deeply staring down at her in agony as He died on a cross.

She doubled her fists and pounded the table in frustrated anger. Then she suddenly stopped and allowed her fingers to caress the scratched and worn wood of the table. Jesus had been a carpenter just like Joseph. What pride He had taken in shaping the wood to His will. As a boy, He had delighted in taking the rough, ugly pieces of wood and turning them into objects for use and of beauty. Sometimes He'd carve beautiful figures out of the scraps and He'd bring them to her saying, "Look, Mama. Nothing is useless to the Father." She would hold Him tightly against her body, cherishing the moment. Once He had pulled away to look up into her eyes and say, "People are a lot like wood, Mama. They just need the Master to work on them."

Her emotion spent for the moment, she lowered her head onto the table. She was glad Joseph had not lived to see Jesus crucified. He too had loved this miraculous, wonderful son. "Dear Father," she moaned, "give me strength to endure and patience to wait until I too can see Your plan. Help—"

A noise from outside the window caused her to raise her head and stare into the early morning light. She could now clearly see the outline of Golgotha through the window. But on the street directly outside there seemed to be a furor of activity.

She rose and stepped to the window. A group of soldiers ran past her little house toward the hill. Villagers were gathering in

47

clusters, individuals breaking away here and there from one group to join another. She could feel the excitement charging the air around them.

"Sir," she called to a merchant who was stepping away from one group, "what has happened?"

"Why it's that Jesus who was crucified just before the Sabbath," he answered.

Feeling the ground swaying beneath her, Mary clutched the windowsill and gasped, "What about Him?"

"Why, He's gone! The women went to the tomb to prepare the body at daybreak this morning, but it wasn't there!"

"Gone? Not there?" she whispered. She looked to the hillside as if expecting to see Jesus walking into the city. "What happened to Him?"

"They *say* His disciples came during the night and stole the body. But ..." the merchant stopped and glanced furtively around him then stepped closer to the window. "But you know what I think?"

Numbly Mary shook her head *no.*

"*I* think He rose from the dead just like He said He would. The women who went to wrap the body came back saying it was gone and that an *angel* told them He had risen from the dead. You know He said once that it'd only take Him three days to rebuild the temple, and that's just what I think He did."

Realizing her knees were buckling beneath her, she turned from the window and allowed her body to sink to the floor. She remained there as the impact of the merchant's words became real to her. "He rose from the dead? He's alive?" Jumping up, she grabbed the tiny box from the table and held it triumphantly in the air above her. "He's alive! He's alive!"

Lifting her face to the heavens, oblivious of the tears that were streaming once again from her eyes, she stretched out her arms and rejoiced in the miracle of God's love. She was finally free from all the doubts and fears she had lived with for so long. Jesus had defeated death. The son God had given her was alive once more.

The first rays of the rising sun pierced through the tiny window casting out the remains of the night. She turned her face toward its light allowing it to warm her skin and laughed into the brilliance of the most beautiful sunrise she had ever known.

MOTHER'S DAY

Mrs. Watts

Mayrene Bobbitt

A Monologue

(Enter a middle-aged woman dressed in colonial costume.)

Good morrow, good Wife Johnston. It's good to see you out to market this bright, sunny day. So glad that you're feeling better of your vapors now. I surely missed you at chapel last meeting day. Oh yes, you missed a fine and unusual service at Above Bar Congregational Church. We celebrated the recent passing by parliament of the Toleration Act. Oh, this Toleration Act of 1689 means a new day for all of us dissenters in the free and independent chapels. Now our members are free to preach and assemble where they like and our men can vote and hold public office.

Why, I remember when I was just a young bride how my own good husband Deacon Watts was thrown in jail three times right here in downtown Southampton. Yes, right in jail, mind you, with all the criminal scum, drunkards, and debtors. And that was just for preaching the gospel in his own neighborhood. I held little Isaac up to the window of that jail to see his father. Yes, it's about time us dissenters are recognized for the good citizens that we are. Now maybe our dedicated congregational young folk will stop this running away across that terrible water to those godforsaken colonies.

Speaking of rebellious young folk, Goody Johnston, did you overhear any of the ruckus that went on at our house after services last Lord's Day? Well, I'm thankful that you did not; I would have been embarrassed to death.

Now our Isaac is usually such a good boy. Never caused me any worry, except over his being so frail and sickly. He gets his lessons so well. Knows his Latin and Greek and French and Hebrew.... Yes, Deacon Watts started teaching him when he was only four years old. He just reads all the time. I'm afraid he'll put his eyes out.

But now Isaac is going on sixteen. And you know how that age is. After services, Isaac began to complain about the doleful psalm singing in our church. Yes, he said it was "dull and boring" and he wasn't going back, mind you. Well, Deacon Watts got so mad, I really feared he'd strike the boy on the Sabbath. The only other time I remember his father getting so mad at young Isaac was when, at about age seven, he was continually making up those rhymes. Everything the boy said just came out in rhymes. Yes, Deacon Watts threatened that if Isaac didn't stop that rhyming he was taking Isaac out behind the shed. Well, little Isaac just looked up so pitiful like and said, "Oh father, do some pity take and I will no more verses make."

Well, this time I knew my good husband was most irritated and impatient over Isaac's complaining about the psalms, for our chapel is quite strict to follow the Calvinist teaching of singing only the metrical psalms. No hymn of "human composure" is allowed. But to my amazement, Deacon Watts in a calm voice just said, "Well then, why don't you give us something better, young man." And you know, Isaac did, too. He sat down that very afternoon and wrote a new hymn which we sang for the evening service. You might just think I'm a bragging mother, but it was good, too. Good as any of those Calvinist psalms. Here's how it starts out:

> Behold the glories of the Lamb
> Amidst His Father's throne;
> Prepare new honors for His name
> And songs before unknown.

Why, thank you, Goody Johnston. I'm glad you like it. Yes, I think my Isaac will make his mark in the world—if husband and I can just live through the next few years!

Happy Mother's Day, Mom!

Enola V. Feldman

A Modern-day Play for Youth

Cast:

CATHY
JAN
BETH
CHRIS
JERRY JONES
JASON JONES
BILLY SMITH
JEAN SMITH
WILMA SMITH

Setting: A utility-type room with shelves of canned goods, a worktable, etc. Cathy, Jan, Chris, and Beth are gathered around the table preparing to fill a large picnic basket.

CATHY: I'm glad Mother said we could go on a picnic today. It's so much fun to visit the park.

JAN: Me too. And I'm glad she invited the Jones twins to come along. Jason and Jerry don't get to do many fun things since their mother died.

BETH: I know. It must be hard trying to get along without a mother. They seem to manage pretty well, though.

CHRIS: That's because they're such big guys. They seem to take care of themselves okay.

JAN: Big, maybe, but they are actually only a couple of months older than I am. That doesn't make them seem big enough to me to be all that self-sufficient!

CHRIS: That's because you're such a big baby.

JAN: Oh, yeah? I'm not as big a baby as you are. At least I can trip over a little old turtle in the yard without screaming my head off!

CATHY: Hey, you two, quit squabbling and help me find the pickles. Mother said we should finish the old jar before opening a new one, but I don't know where it is.

(All turn to shelves to look.)

BETH: I hope there are enough left to go around. You know, we asked the Smith gang to come, too. They're bringing the potato salad. *(Puts hands on hips.)* Now, where can that jar of pickles be? We had some only yesterday.

(Knock on door.)

CATHY: Maybe that's Mother back from the library. She said she'd be back soon.

BETH *(opening door):* It's the other guys. Come in, come in.

(Smith and Jones children troop in.)

WILMA: Here's the potato salad. *(Places bowl on table.)*

JERRY: We brought some fresh carrots. They're homegrown in California, where our cousin lives. He sent them last week.

JASON: Dad says they must have had a lot of rain to make them grow fast. I'm glad it doesn't look like rain here today.

JAN: I'll say. Mother wouldn't take us to the park if it even looked like it. I guess she thinks we're marshmallows or something.

CHRIS: Nobody'd mistake *you* for a marshmallow! A horseradish, maybe, but never a marshmallow.

(Jan makes a face at Chris.)

CATHY: What is the matter with you two today? If you'd get busy looking for those pickles, you wouldn't be in each other's hair.

JAN: Oh, yes, the pickles!

(Everyone looks high and low.)

BILLY *(pointing to row of pickle jars):* There they are, top shelf.

CATHY *(shaking head):* Those haven't been opened. We have to use the jar that's partly gone first.

JEAN: Well, if the jar has been opened, it's probably in the refrigerator.

CATHY: Of course! Why didn't I think of that? I'll go look right now. *(Exits.)*

JASON: How come you are working out here instead of in the kitchen?

CHRIS: Mother was scrubbing the floor there when we started. She put a throw rug down in front of the refrigerator, but she didn't want a mess everywhere else. It should be dry by now. You see, Gramps and Grandma and Aunt Sally's family are coming tomorrow—

JASON: Oh, Mother's Day! *(Exchanges sad look with Jerry.)*

BILLY *(brightly, as if to change the subject):* I noticed you had a little booklet with you, Jerry. Is it a new paperback we haven't read yet?

JERRY *(taking booklet from pocket):* Do you mean this? It has our Sunday-school lessons in it. We have already studied for Sunday, but we thought some of you might check us out on the answers.

BILLY: Sure thing. Let's see it.

CATHY *(coming back with pickles):* You were right, Jean. The jar was in the refrigerator.

JAN *(opening loaf of bread):* Well, I hope you also brought the lunch meat and the eggs. They were in there too.

CATHY: Nope. I just brought pickles. You said pickles, so I looked for pickles and brought pickles. You need mayonnaise and other junk for the sandwiches anyhow. You can get them.

JAN: Okay, but I'll need help.

JEAN: I can help you. *(They exit.)*

BETH: I wish Mother had made the sandwiches. Jan never puts on enough mayonnaise.

WILMA: I'll spread the bread then. I like it good and thick too. *(Sniffs.)* Say, do you smell something burning?

CATHY: It must be the pies! I forgot all about them. Mother told me to watch them in case she didn't get right back. *(Cathy and Wilma run out.)*

JASON: Your mother made pies for our picnic?

CHRIS: Yep, fresh apple pies! And she made a dreamy chocolate cake for tomorrow. Mother loves to bake. And we love to eat.

(Girls come back with eggs, mayonnaise, and lunch meat.)

CATHY: Good news! The pies were not burned, just the juice that bubbled over. Who wants to devil the eggs?

JERRY AND JASON *(together):* I will!

CATHY: Good. Chris and Wilma can make the sandwiches. Jan and Jean mix up our fruit drink. Billy, you can collect the paper napkins, plates, and spoons we will need. I'll arrange the things in the basket. How's that?

BETH: Fine, I guess, but you didn't give me a job.

CATHY: You can wipe off the table when we're through, okay?

BETH: Okay.

JASON: Meanwhile, why don't you turn to the questions in our lesson and see how many we can answer?

JERRY: Yeah! The lesson is about mothers, you'll notice.

BETH: Page twenty. Here it is. Ready? Maybe I'd better get my Bible first.

JERRY: Ready. Yes, you may need to refer to Proverbs.

BETH: "What makes you think Naomi was a good mother?" That's the first question.

JASON: That's easy. Because Ruth would not have loved her enough to leave her own country to be with Naomi. Unless she was an awfully nice mother-in-law, Ruth would have stayed with her own people.

BETH: Right. Jerry, this one is for you. "Naomi was a virtuous woman. Tell how Proverbs describes a virtuous woman."

JERRY: Well, for one thing, she works hard. She gets up before daylight to start the family's meals.

JASON: And she not only gets clothes for her own family, she gives things to the poor.

CATHY: Our mother does that, too. When the Andersons had that fire, she went through our closets and made up a bundle of good clothes we didn't wear anymore or had outgrown. I think our mother must be a virtuous woman.

BILLY: She surely does a lot of nice things for people.

BETH: Is there anything else?

JERRY: Oh, a virtuous woman is careful about buying things for her household. She doesn't waste her husband's money.

BETH: You are right. Say, I think Mother meets that qualification, too. She goes to lots of sales, but even if the price is low, she doesn't buy things unless they are of good quality and things we really need. She always says, "A bargain is not a bargain if you don't need it."

JASON: I know another. A virtuous woman does not do a lot of chattering just to be talking. She says smart things that mean something.

BETH (checking down list): Let's see here. Yes, it does say that, in the twenty-sixth verse. "She speaks with wisdom, and faithful instruction is on her tongue."

BILLY: She's a good businesswoman, too. It says in there somewhere that she looks at a field and buys it.

CATHY: She does? I didn't think women were allowed to do things like that then.

BETH: Yes, it's so.

CATHY: Mother bought some land once. Remember?

CHRIS: Yeah, and she later sold it for twice as much. That new complex on Stafford and Elm needed her lot to finish building the complex.

CATHY *(grinning):* Dad kidded her about being a business tycoon, but you could tell he was really proud of her.

JAN: She didn't want the money for herself, either. She wrote a check for our missionary in Korea, and then she put the rest of it into bonds for our college educations.

JERRY *(thoughtfully):* A virtuous woman is so good and kind that her children "arise and call her blessed."

JASON: And her husband praises her.

BETH: Good. I think that question is pretty well answered. Now for another. "Name three women in the Bible who might meet this standard of virtue."

JERRY: Would Hannah be one? She gave Samuel to the Lord when he was still a child, but she made clothes for him and went to visit him.

BETH: I would think so.

JASON: How about Eunice and Lois? The apostle Paul said that Timothy was lucky to have a mother and grandmother like they were.

BILLY: Don't forget Mary, the mother of Jesus. She must have set a good example for Him when He was young.

JEAN: And Elizabeth, the mother of John the Baptist, too.

BETH: Well, that's more than three already, and there must be dozens more. Let's get on to the next one. "Think of ways to honor your mother." Oh, I guess you don't need to answer that.

JERRY: Sure we do. Jason and I can honor our mother by trying to be the kind of boys she wanted us to be when she was alive.

JASON: She was a nice person, very much like your mother, Beth. She liked picnics too.

JERRY: She sure did! She was a lot of fun, like yours. By the way, we don't want to forget to thank your mother for letting us go with you today. Not everyone would take a gang for an outing when she is expecting company the next day.

CHRIS: Well, that's Mother for you.

BILLY: We want to thank her for letting us come, too.

CATHY: We're glad you all could come. Picnics are more fun when more people are there.

CHRIS: Yeah, and the more people, the more food!

JEAN: Your mother is not only a fun person, she's a good Sunday-school teacher, too.

WILMA: To my way of thinking, you have one of the nicest mothers in town—next to ours of course.

CATHY: We agreed, don't we? *(Jan, Chris, and Beth nod heads.)* The only thing about it is, we hardly ever tell her how we feel. Maybe we should.

JAN: Tomorrow's Mother's Day. We always tell her how special we think she is then.

BETH: We tell her. This year maybe we could do something more.

CHRIS: More? What else is there?

JAN: Well, we could act more loving. You and I, we do a lot of squabbling, right? We might try cooling that.

CHRIS: But she would think we were sick if we did that!

BETH: Oh, I think Jan has a point. We could make Mother happier. Take our chores, for instance. We could do them a lot faster than we do, and with a lot less griping and fooling around.

JAN: Sure we could. She always expects us to be pretty good on Mother's Day. Why don't we surprise her this year and make *every day* Mother's Day?

CHRIS: Hey, now, let's not get carried away with these resolutions. It's quite a strain for me to be decent for just one day.

JAN: It would still be for just one day. One day at a time, anyhow. If we pray about it, we can make it.

CHRIS: Okay, if you put it that way. I'm game to try if the rest of you are.

CATHY: What about it, gang? *(Jan and Beth nod.)* It's unanimous! We can start today by wishing Mother a happy yearlong Mother's Day.

JAN *(looking out window):* Beginning right now. She's coming up the walk. Is everybody ready?

(All rush to door shouting "Happy Mother's Day.")

Curtain

FATHER'S DAY

The Best Gift

Helen Kitchell Evans

A Playlet for Boys

Cast:

BOB	BEN
JACK	JAMES
JASON	PETE
TOM	MR. ALLEN
HARRY	

(When the scene opens they are seated in a circle around a campfire. They are talking.)

BOB: Next week is Father's Day. I just don't know what to give my dad for Father's Day. I don't have much money saved and things cost so very much.

JACK: Remember, it isn't the gift but the thought that counts.

JASON: Yes, my dad was more pleased one time with a little pencil holder I made at school than he ever was with a new shirt.

TOM: Why is that? Seems to me I'd rather have the new shirt.

HARRY: Me, too! I like new clothes.

BEN: Maybe we will know someday when we are grown and get to be fathers.

JAMES: I suppose we will, but I can't see either how some little old pencil box could mean so much. My dad felt the same way about a letter holder I made for him. I was in the first grade then, and he still keeps that old thing on his desk. I could do much better now.

PETE: One day my mother said something that might be the reason why dads hold on to things like that. She said that next to God's love no love is greater than a parent for his child. They love us so much that anything we do that is thoughtful makes them proud of us.

JACK: I have an idea. Let's all plan to make something here at camp that we could give our dads for Father's Day. I wonder if Mr. Allen would let us.

HARRY: I'm sure he would. He's almost like a second father, especially when we're away from home.

PETE: I'll go get him. *(He leaves and returns with Mr. Allen.)*

MR. ALLEN: Pete tells me that you have a plan to present to me.

BOB: Yes, we do. I was wondering what to give my dad for Father's Day and we all began to talk about what to do.

TOM: Now we have decided to see if we can make something here at camp for our fathers.

MR. ALLEN: I think that is a great idea. I had a plan in mind for you, but I'm happy to see you think for yourselves and come to me with the idea before I had to come to you.

JAMES: That's fine. What did you plan to do?

MR. ALLEN: Well, let's hear some of your ideas first. You don't all have to do the same thing, you know.

BOB: I'd like to make a tie rack.

JACK: I'd like to make a little dog paperweight. My dad is so fond of our dog that I think he would like that.

JASON: I'd like to make a pencil holder. You know, one with a lot of small holes in the top to hold lots of pencils on his desk.

TOM: Pass me. I have to think a little while.

HARRY: Could I make a footstool?

MR. ALLEN: I think so, with some help.

BEN: I want to make a leather holder for Dad's tools, one that would roll up so he could carry it with him.

JAMES: That's a good idea. I'd like that, too.

PETE: I'm like Tom. I need to think a while longer.

MR. ALLEN: Well, let's think some more tomorrow. It's about vesper time. I just want to tell you boys how proud I am of you. Every year when I come to camp I find out that all boys are good.

BEN: My dad says all boys are good if they have good parents and good leaders to help them grow up.

MR. ALLEN: Your father is a very wise man. Fathers need the cooperation of their boys, though. If a boy wants to please his father he can do it by obeying him.

PETE: I guess you could say then, that it doesn't matter so much what we make for him for a gift. Our *best* gift is obedience and a willingness to do the right thing.

MR. ALLEN: That's exactly correct. Let's go to vespers now, boys.

Curtain

PENTECOST

The Fulfillment of Promise

Enola V. Feldman

A Pentecost Program

Prelude: "Go to the Deeps" (instrumental)
Welcome:

> We have come today to celebrate
> A custom very old,
> Yet one whose meaning brings new joy
> Each time it is retold.
>
> So open wide your inmost hearts.
> Let gladness enter there,
> Then know the peace that comes when God
> Has blessed you in your prayer.

Leader: Jesus was a man of prayer. He communed always with God, always bowing to His Father's will. We also know His knowledge of the Old Testament, especially the prophecies of Isaiah and Jeremiah, helped guide His daily life. As the Messiah, He had power to heal the sick, open the eyes of the blind, unstop the ears of the deaf, and raise the dead. All this was foretold by these prophets. He proved how God was true to His many promises. Because of this, Jesus could reassure His followers by saying, "Do not think that I have come to abolish the Law or the Prophets; I have not come to abolish them but to fulfill them" (Matthew 5:17).

Song: "Claim the Promise" (mixed quartet)

Leader: One of the laws Jesus did not break was the observance of Pentecost which was first initiated by Moses at God's command.

Scripture Reading: Leviticus 23:15-21

Leader: Although the Jews had faithfully celebrated this Feast of Weeks at the close of this harvest each year, many gave only lip service to God. Unrighteous practices had sprung up, perpetrated even by the priests and Pharisees. Jesus warned the people about them, trying every way He knew to purify their hearts. He saw how badly they needed to be turned back to the true worship of their Creator. He also had compassion on sinners in Samaria. He called the souls of all mankind "ripe for harvest."

Scripture Reading: John 4:35-39

Leader: The harvest Jesus most wanted to garner was the changed attitudes of His own generation of Jews. When many refused to listen, He opened the door to the Gentiles. To you and me! This too was foretold by the prophets.

Scripture Reading: Isaiah 49:6

Leader: That was another of God's promises kept.

Song: "I Know God's Promise Is True" (mixed quartet)

Leader: Jesus' timing was always perfect, and in keeping with God's ordinances. He, knowing full well He would be the sacrificial lamb, observed the Passover with His disciples in Jerusalem. Before His crucifixion, He warned His followers what would happen. All through the mockery of a trial and His resultant mistreatment, He remembered Isaiah's prophecy, conducting himself accordingly.

Scripture Reading: Isaiah 50:6, 7

Leader: Jesus' love for God and His love for the world was so great He scarcely spoke when Pilate questioned Him. He refused to give the Romans an excuse for setting Him free, because He knew that only by His death could He save mankind. Again Jesus was adhering to prophecy, fulfilling God's promise.

Scripture Reading: Isaiah 53:3-8

Leader: He paid the penalty for all of us who believe in Him.

Song: "Nailed to the Cross" (mixed quartet)

Leader: Of course the sacrifice of Jesus would serve little purpose if it were not known outside of Judea. The incident would have to be boldly told by eyewitnesses. You see, dying was only half of Isaiah's prophecy. The most miraculous part, Christ's resurrection, was also foretold. The world would have to hear about it. But who would tell? The disciples were disillusioned, frightened, and hopeless.

Scripture Reading: Isaiah 26:19

Leader: When Christ, triumphant over death, walked in newness of life with His scattered flock, they again united to do the Master's will. His new command was to wait together for the empowering gift of the Holy Spirit. This did not come immediately after their Lord's ascension into Heaven, however. Again, the appropriate time was set for a Jewish holy season. It was on the sixth of Sivan, or Pentecost, when the people celebrated the end of their harvest, that Jesus sent the Comforter to His harvesters. What joy! What power! What great deeds they could now do for the glory of God! We read this account in Acts.

Scripture Reading: Acts 2:1-6

Leader: And so the Gospel of the risen Messiah was fearlessly preached. When persecution came, the faithful continued to give their testimony. Some were put in jail. That did not silence them. Still other were forced to flee to foreign lands, but they took the Gospel with them, converting many. Some gave their most vivid witness as they were brought to their own executions. The disheartened apostles had become new creatures, transformed by the Holy Spirit. Christendom was born!

Song: "The Church's One Foundation" (congregation)

Leader: The Holy Spirit baptized the disciples with spiritual tongues of fire. The Scriptures tell us He will come individually to all who truly believe and seek His comfort. Jeremiah foretold this wonder generations before Christ's birth.

Scripture Reading: Jeremiah 32:38-40

Leader: John the Baptist also proclaimed it.

Scripture Reading: Luke 3:16

Leader: God's promises and prophecies were and are still being fulfilled. Jesus was true to them. By His actions and life, He unfolded God's redemptive plan. His church was a part of it. You may be sure it will endure to the end of time, for Jesus our Lord assured His apostles and us, "And surely I will be with you always, to the very end of the age." We who believe this will listen to the promptings of His Spirit in our hearts and follow wherever it directs.

Song: "Lead On, O King Eternal" (congregation)

Benediction: O Heavenly Father, we pray that the fire that baptized the first apostles in Jerusalem may burn the sins from our hearts now. May it empower us all to stand firm against temptation. Fill us with Your love. This we ask not only in Your name, but in the name of Jesus our Redeemer, and that of the Holy Spirit you sent to enlighten our way. Amen.

Postlude: "The Comforter Has Come" (instrumental)

A Mighty,

Rushing Wind

Florence Harper Haney

Oh, mighty rushing wind,
Oh, power of God's Spirit,
New life is breathed upon
Our souls if we will hear it.

Oh, tongue of flame and fire,
Oh, glory from above,
Christ promised You would come
To light our lives with love.

Amazed, we feel the presence
Of the power from on high.
Oh, God, that power will keep us
If on You we will rely.